Istanbul Is Mystery Babylon

The Bible Prophecy Investigated

By: Ernest Serano

ISBN 9781792697104

Contents

Introduction

The biblical book of Revelation (also referred to as The Apocalypse) contains many prophecies that will take place near the very end of the last days we are in. Among those prophecies is the destruction of a major international city which is spiritually called *Great Babylon* and also *Mystery Babylon the Great*. So key is this event that about four chapters in the Revelation deal with it.

My written work here will lay out the case for the identity of Mystery Babylon based on the narrative about it in the Revelation, the last book of the Bible. Probably the most popular guess as to the identity of Mystery Babylon has been the city of Rome. However, that is not the conclusion that will be put forth here. Neither New York nor Mecca make the cut either. Reasons for dismissing those cities will be mentioned later.

While I will not be adamant that my understanding of the identity of Mystery Babylon is 100% correct and that there could be no other alternative for it, I am about 99% sure it is the correct choice. Until a more compelling case is put forth, I will stand and promote my position on this subject.

I expect that the evidence and commentary I present on this subject will be new to just about all of the readers of this work for the simple fact that I have not come across a similar view presented by anyone, as of the time of this writing. I suspect that someone or another has probably came to the same basic conclusion as I have on the identity of Mystery Babylon but has not been as public about it, at least not in the internet searches I have done.

My aim is to not deal with an exhaustive narrative on Mystery Babylon but to center mostly on its identity. I will make the case in this work that Mystery Babylon is the city of Istanbul located in the country of Turkey. Istanbul fits all of the major biblical narrative about the great city as described in scripture and then some.

A major clue was found about Mystery Babylon while I was reading a novel. That clue was practically earth shattering to me and became the stimulus for me to start investigating Mystery Babylon again. Actually, it was more like an electrical shock that moved me to action. It just goes to show you that you can learn some very interesting background information is some novels.

Like a detective on a cold case, that first big clue blew the case wide open. That big clue then led me to another major clue and then everything seemed to fall into place after that.

I had read the biblical passages concerning Mystery Babylon many times over the years but until recently, I had overlooked that second major clue and realized that it seems that everyone else also misses it as they don't comment on it in their description of the great city. Those two big clues will be mentioned later in this book and you will see what an enormous help they were to nail down the location of this great city.

And now, it would be best to cover some background on Mystery Babylon to better understand its setting and why that name is probably used.

Chapter 1- Babylon

Mystery Babylon is a spiritual name, no doubt corresponding to the ancient Babylon of Iraq that was one of the first great cities of mankind mentioned in the book of Genesis and known for being the location of the famed Tower of Babel.

Many of the biblical accounts of Babylon take place around the time of Jeremiah who was a prophet and priest of Israel (he was around since the early 7th century B.C.) The similarities to Mystery Babylon and ancient Babylon are very close.

Ancient Babylon was the heart of the great Babylonian empire that ruled and had influence over much of the world then. Later on, that empire would be attacked by the kings of the Medes and the Persians.

The book of Jeremiah (chapter 51 verse 7) tells us that Babylon was a golden cup that made the earth drunk with her wine. God's plan for Babylon was to destroy it with His vengeance for plundering Israel and taking its people captive (Jerimiah 51:49). That was how Daniel the prophet came to write his book in Babylon as he had been taken captive there.

Jeremiah warns people to flee Babylon due to its coming judgment. He goes on to foretell that Babylon will be left "desolate forever" (Jeremiah 51:26). Indeed, since Babylon was destroyed; it has never been rebuilt and repopulated as a city.

The late Saddam Hussein, who ruled Iraq, set out to rebuild Babylon but his efforts were short lived and Babylon remains fairly desolate today. He actually believed he would be another great Babylonian King as the biblical king Nebuchadnezzar was and directed that a couple of palaces in Babylon be rebuilt. He had three modest "palaces" built but with the war that went on with a coalition of nations against Iraq, and his eventual capture and demise, not much of anything else got done.

It turned out that Saddam had wreaked havoc on ancient ruins by building over them and destroying some parts of them with his new construction. A 2003 article in the "Marines", official website of the United States Marine Corps, details this in an article by Sgt. Colin Wyers titled, *Hussein 'ruined' ruins of Babylon."*

In Revelation chapters 17-19, we have a parallel scenario for Mystery Babylon. The great city also has a golden cup from which the nations have drunk the wine of wrath of her fornication. God also calls His people to come out of her to avoid her plagues and judgment. Her destruction will also come by a coalition of nations that attack her ultimately as God's vengeance for persecuting His people. Mystery Babylon will be desolate and found no more (Rev 18:21). As Ecclesiastics states, "there is nothing new under the sun" (Ecc 1: 9).

Chapter 2- History

It is said that Istanbul is the only city in the world located on two continents (Europe and Asia). Some background on Istanbul and Turkey will help understand the current situation there.

The ancient name for the country of Turkey was Anatolia. It became Turkey in 1923. Turkey from the Middle Latin means "land of the Turks." Istanbul's most ancient name was Byzantium believed to have been founded around 657 B.C.

About 1,000 years after Byzantium was founded it was taken over by the Romans under Emperor Constantine and renamed Constantinople (after his name). In 330 A.D. Constantine made Constantinople the new capital of the Roman Empire instead of Rome. It was often referred to as the "New Rome"

Constantine converted to Christianity and some churches and cathedrals were built in Constantinople. That is not that surprising when one considers a particular aspect of ancient Turkey. Ancient Turkey was one of the first countries outside of Israel that was evangelized with the Gospel of Jesus Christ. A key verse on this is in Revelation 1:4 where the apostle John addresses his letter as, "John, to the seven churches in Asia." All seven of those churches; Ephesus, Smyrna, Pergamos, Thyatira, Sardis, Philadelphia and Laodicea were located in ancient Turkey.

Constantinople also became the capital of the Byzantine Empire also known as the Eastern Roman Empire. It was renowned for being a great walled city with much splendor. Byzantium and later as Constantinople, ruled empires and nations for well over a millennium.

Constantinople superseded Rome as the new capital of the Roman Empire. The city of Rome eventually lost its might and influence over much of the world as it fell in 476 A.D. This became the end of the Western Roman Empire. Constantinople would reign as the Eastern Roman Empire for several more centuries.

Chapter 3- Desert or Wilderness

We have been in the Last Days, since the day of Pentecost in the book of Acts of the New Testament. The apostle Peter told us in Acts 2:16-17 that the outpouring of the Holy Spirit on Pentecost was the fulfillment of the Old Testament. Peter quoted the prophet Joel and spoke of what had happened then as having "come to pass in the last days." Now after more than two thousand years since that day of Pentecost, we are so much further into the last days that we are nearing the end part of those days.

I must note here that when the apostle John is shown the judgment of Mystery Babylon in the "wilderness" (Rev 17:3) that it does not mean that the literal location of Mystery Babylon is in a wilderness. Most Bibles use the word "wilderness" or "desert" but either way they are most likely referring to just where John had his vision and not the literal location of Mystery Babylon. We can understand this better by reading on.

In Rev 17:3 the Greek word used for wilderness or desert is erēmon which according to Strong's Concordance on the Greek language is an adjective meaning deserted or desolate not a noun which are how the words wilderness and desert are usually used in the scripture just mentioned.

I am dwelling on this area because some people state that Mystery Babylon is located in a desert or wilderness based on a general translation Bibles often use in that passage and miss the more accurate meaning just explained here. This was new to me as well until I happened to look it up. As the saying goes, "enquiring minds want to know."

Another example of the spiritual in contrast to a literal understanding is when Jesus was taken up by the Devil onto a high mountain and shown "all the kingdoms of the world" (Mat 4:8). In the next verse, the devil promised to give Jesus all that he was being shown if he would fall down and worship him.

It is physically impossible to see "all the kingdoms of the world" even from the highest mountain in the world, Mt Everest, which is, 29,029 feet or 8,848 meters above sea level. There is a mathematical formula to figure out how far a person can see standing at sea level and beyond from elevated heights. That math makes out that if a person was standing at 32,800 feet or 10,000 meters, which is higher than Mount Everest, they would see out to about 214 miles or 357 meters.

Clearly "all the kingdoms of the world" are not located within 214 miles of any mountain in Israel or any place else in the world for that matter. At a distance of 214 miles one would still be inside most countries with the vast majority of the world unseen.

So, what Jesus saw on the mountain where the devil took him was not a natural location where "all the kingdoms of the world" can be seen. It was more like a vision.

It would seem rather obvious that any great city would not be located in an isolated or lonely place as in a wilderness or desert just by the mere fact that such a great city would be heavily populated and visited by many others going and coming to it as well.

Apart from dreams, it seems that biblically when a person has a vision; it is usually away from largely populated places and that could be why John was taken to a deserted place to have his vison.

Chapter 4- Four Major Clues

In Revelation 17:1-6, the apostle John is introduced to the "judgment of the great harlot who sits on many waters, with whom the kings of the earth committed fornications, and the inhabitants of the earth were made drunk with the wine of her fornication".

Revelation 17: 15 relates that the waters that John saw where the harlot sits are "peoples, multitudes, nations and tongues." That description fits a large international city as is the case with Istanbul which has one of the densest populations of all cities in the world with over 2,500 people per square kilometer

John goes on to say in that chapter that he saw "a woman sitting on a scarlet beast which was full of names of blasphemy, having seven heads and ten horns." She was "arrayed in purple and scarlet, and adorned with gold and precious stones and pearls, having in her hand a golden cup full of abominations and the filthiness of her fornication.

Furthermore, "on her forehead a name was written: MYSTERY, BABYLON THE GREAT, THE MOTHER OF HARLOTS AND OF THE ABOMINATIONS OF THE EARTH." John also sees that the woman "was drunk with the blood of the saints and with the martyrs of Jesus."

Chapter 17:12-17 also states that John is told that ten kings join together and under an authority called "the beast" (generally understood to be the Antichrist, a world ruler that will make himself out to be as God himself) and attack the harlot, Mystery Babylon, and burn her with fire as a judgment upon her, ultimately from God.

The scripture relates that this destruction is due to her abominations and murder of his saints (more on these two areas will be dealt with in later chapters).

Some of the narrative just covered is symbolic but we get some interpretation for it from passages in Revelation. Chapter 17 verse 18 tells us that "the woman whom you saw is that great city which reigns over the kings of the earth." This is the literal and valid interpretation of what the "woman" represents. It is common for some people to say that Mystery Babylon is: a church (often associated with the Roman Catholic Church), a political system or a country such as America, but, to do so is to ignore the scripture.

Above all else, the "woman" is a city. Not just any city either but a "great" city. That eliminates most cities as any city not great would tend to be more mundane and unexceptional rather than noteworthy. This is the first major clue given on this subject.

Next, consider another major clue as to the location of that great city. Revelation 17, verse 9 states, "here is the mind which has wisdom: the seven heads are seven mountains on which the woman sits." The seven heads were first mentioned back in Revelation 17: 3 where it stated that the woman sat on a beast having seven heads.

This additional second big clue, that the great city is located on seven mountains, which is sometimes also translated as seven hills, really narrows down a location for the great city. Any city not known for containing 7 notable hills can be disregarded from being a candidate for being Mystery Babylon.

A third clue about the city is that it is also a city that persecuted and killed Christians and may do so in the future (see Revelation 17:6). After Mystery Babylon is judged and destroyed, there is rejoicing in heaven for the vengeance God has poured on her for killing holy apostles, prophets and his saints (Revelation 18:20, 19:1-3). The great city has blood on its hands and awaits God's judgment.

A fourth major clue is that the great city is known for world trade including sea trade (Rev 18:17). All of these major clues will be covered in more detail in the chapters that follow.

Chapter 5- A Great City

Istanbul has long ago outgrown its original walls. That great city has truly become even greater in size. Depending on what world statistics one looks at, it is fairly accurate to say that Istanbul is one of the world's top ten largest cities! After reviewing multiple population statistics on Istanbul, it seems very reasonable that it is more likely to be the seventh most populated city in the world with a population now of about 15 million people! I think most people, especially in the West, do not realize how big this city is.

For comparison; New York City (actual city limits) is about 8.6 million close to being half as populated as Istanbul. Rome's population is about 3 million making Istanbul five times more populated than it and Mecca (which is in Saudi Arabia) has a main population of about 1.6 million making Istanbul at least nine times more populated than it is.

I mention New York, Rome and Mecca since these three cities are often cited as locations for Mystery Babylon but they do not come even close to the greatness of population and size to Istanbul.

While Mecca is considered an international city, only Muslims are allowed there as it is a most holy city of Islam. The population and geography of Mecca alone does not make it stand out from similar cities of the same size as a very great city. It really gets its fame as being the birth place of Mohamed and the annual pilgrimage to it by the Moslem faithful.

Chapter 6- Seven Hills

There are two main reasons that Constantine made Constantinople his new Rome. One reason for that being that it was centrally located to the whole Roman Empire. The other reason, which also relates to the identity of Mystery Babylon, is that the city was located on seven hills just as Rome was!

This geographical likeness to Rome is probably the most notable feature as to its identity. This is the key clue I had discovered in a novel I had read where it was stated that Constantinople had been built on seven hills.

All of these seven hills are located inside where the original walls of Constantinople were. In fact, in that part of the world, Istanbul is known as "the city on the seven hills" which in Turkish is "Yedi tepeli sehir."

Various online sites mention the seven hills and their locations so I have put a list of them here in order from the first to the last.

The first hill on which the original city of Byzantium was founded originates from *Seraglio Point* and includes the great Hagia Sophia, once a Christian cathedral but now a public museum. The Sultan Ahmed Mosque and Topkapi Palace is also in that area

The second hill includes the location of the *Column of Constantine* which was originally 50 meters high and supported a great statue of Emperor Constantine which fell and was greatly damaged so long ago.

The third hill contains the main buildings of Istanbul University, the Bayezid II Mosque to the south and the Süleymaniye Mosque to the north.

The fourth hill has the Fatih Mosque on it, formerly the location of the Church of the Holy Apostles that was built on order of Emperor Constantine.

The fifth hill contains the Yavuz Sultan Selim Mosque, a   16th-century Ottoman imperial mosque almost 500 year old now.

On the sixth hill can be found the Mihrimah Sultan Mosque near the highest point of the city, the mosque is a prominent landmark in Istanbul.

Last of all, the seventh hill extends to the Theodosian Wall and on to the Mamara Sea. The walls were the largest and strongest ever built in either the ancient or medieval worlds, probably excluding the Great Wall of China. Only certain sections still remain now.

The popularity of the seven hills in Istanbul is also attested to by a popular hotel there called *Seven Hills Hotel* located near the older part of Istanbul. It boasts spectacular views of the area including a rooftop seafood restaurant where night views are especially sought to see the lighted city around it and the nearby sea.

Chapter 7- Judgement Awaits

We will now cover Revelation 17:6 that mentions why Mystery Babylon will be destroyed. This has to do with how she has been "drunk with the blood of the saints and blood of the martyrs."

In review, God stirs up a coalition of nations to attack and burn down Mystery Babylon as he exacts revenge on it for persecuting and murdering his people (Revelation 17:16-17 and 18:5-8). You will understand that there is a shocking history of great bloodletting by the hands of Mystery Babylon against Christians as you read on.

From the time that Constantinople became the new Rome, around 324 AD, many churches and some great cathedrals were built throughout the Roman Empire and especially in that great city. The church that flourished in Constantinople was the Eastern Orthodox Church rather than the Western or Spanish Catholic Church.

One of the Eastern Church's greatest cathedrals often spoken of as being one of the most magnificent buildings ever built in the world is The Hagia Sophia, built in Constantinople.

Constantinople remained the capital of the Roman Empire and later the Eastern Roman Empire which was referred to as the Byzantine Empire until 1453. The Roman Empire eventually collapsed and was taken over by enemies until only the great city of Constantinople was left standing.

The Ottoman Turks, who were Muslims, took over most of the Byzantine Empire and in 1453 besieged Constantinople. With an armada of ships the Turks assaulted the sea side of the city eventually breaching the sea walls to the city. Besides that, the Turks used newer larger cannons which were rather formidable and inflicted significant damage to the great wall surrounding the city. With no help from outside sources, Constantinople fell. What followed was a blood bath.

In the book *"Constantinople- City of the World's desire,"* written by Phillip Mansel, he records an eyewitness account of that terrible day in his first chapter. "Blood flowed through the streets like rain water after a sudden storm, corpses floated out to sea like melons along a canal."

The Turkish troops pillaged, plundered and massacred for 3 days. Many people, who sought refuge in the churches, including the Hagia Sophia, were butchered there. Nuns were raped. Most of the Nobles were killed. It is estimated that 30,000 Christian inhabitants were enslaved and deported.

Eventually the cathedrals were turned into mosques. The Hagia Sophia is now a museum open to visitors and a prime tourist spot with paid admission. After the defeat of Constantinople, the Ottoman Empire would last for about 500 years with that city now its Muslim capital. Constantinople, taken over by a Muslim invasion by the Turks, became a city that persecuted the Church there and would be on God's list of remembrance.

In 1915 the Ottoman Empire was still around with Constantinople as its capital. In that year, the tragic and horrible event known as the Armenian Genocide occurred. The Armenian's homeland was one of the first nations to convert to Christianity so they were Christians.

The current Republic of Armenia lies along the North East side of Turkey above the north tip of Iran. Long ago before it was a Republic, the ancient Kingdom of Armenia encompassed a significant portion of Turkey. For that reason there had been a very large Armenian population in Turkey up to the time the genocide began.

The genocide had its impetus from World War 1 that started in 1914. The government of Turkey was fearful that its Armenian population would turn on it and join against it in the war as some enemy troops contained Armenians. At first some Armenians were rounded up for deportation but that turned out to be an excuse to start killing them in mass. Soon the killing was openly committed.

Death squads roamed around, some victims were actually crucified on large crosses and other victims were buried alive. Death marches to the desert took place where the victims, many being women, had no food or water and died. Women were raped, children were taken and raised Muslim and some victims were enslaved.

Another motive for the genocide appears to have been economic gain. While most of those Armenians were citizens and paid taxes, confiscation of their properties and wealth took place. In some cases victims were told to completely disrobe before being killed so that their clothing could be saved for sale.

It is estimated that between 1 million to 1 ½ million Armenians were slaughtered. The hundred year anniversary of that genocide occurred in 2015. To this day, the government of Turkey does not acknowledge that it committed this atrocity even though it is well documented. The scripture tells us that vengeance is God's (Romans 12:19) and he will take some of that vengeance when Mystery Babylon is destroyed.

In May of 2018, the President of Turkey, Erdogan, projected a plan of uniting Islamic countries to overthrow Israel and free Palestine. Socially there is a growing persecution against churches in Turkey as well although being a Christian is not currently outlawed and Sharia Law is not in force, 98% of the population is Muslim. In 2016, the government seized control of six churches in the city of Diyarbakir claiming it is rebuilding the area but church worshipers there fear a coup against them.

Chapter 8- World Trade

This is a very important chapter in understanding how well Istanbul fits the narrative about Mystery Babylon. We will consider the major feature of Mystery Babylon which I had alluded to in the introduction as being always overlooked. This great city is an international trade center known for being a major sea port to the world!

We have a hint of this in Revelation 17:4 where we are told the woman (the city Mystery Babylon) is "adorned with gold, precious stones and *pearls*." Trade in pearls would suggest that there is a close proximity to ocean waters. Trade in pearls is also mentioned in Rev 18:12,16.

Revelation 18:3 mentions that "the merchants of the earth have become rich through the abundance of her luxury." So great is Mystery Babylon a trade center that about all of the rest of Revelation 18 deals with this narrative. Merchants of the earth weep and mourn over Mystery Babylon because no one buys their merchandise anymore.

The main way this trade is conducted is by ships coming and going to the great city from locations in different parts of the world such as Africa, the Middle East and Asia as inferred by some of the details of Rev 18:12-13.

This merchandise is specifically listed as "gold and silver, precious stones, pearls, fine linen and purple, silk and scarlet, every kind of citron wood, every kind of object of ivory, every kind of object of most precious wood, bronze, iron, marble: and cinnamon and incense, fragrant oil and frankincense, wine and oil, fine flour and wheat, cattle and sheep, horses and chariots, and bodies and souls of men (per the UN Office of Drugs and Crime, Turkey is a major destination for human trafficking).

In Revelation 18:17-18 it states that "every shipmaster, all who travel by ship, sailors, and as many as trade on the sea," will lament the destruction that happens when the great city is destroyed in one hour. This is so clear that a seaport city is being talked about that to miss it makes one think that a veil was over one's eyes.

There are four references to sea trade in the previous paragraph and it does not take much imagination to picture cargo ships, oil tankers, cruise ships and various military ships in those waters.

Also, those witnesses who see the destruction of the city will ask, "What is like this great city?" This also lets us know that this is a unique city not comparable to other cities.

And finally in Revelation 18:19, those witnesses cry and wail over the great city saying, "All who had ships on the sea became rich by her wealth!" Here is another significant reference to a seaport city and great trade being done there.

Istanbul is a great international sea port as it is located near bodies of water involving world trade directly to Europe and Asia. To the north is The Black Sea, accessed by a strait through upper Istanbul known as The Bosporus which one marine archeologist has called "the greatest natural harbor in the world," that can accommodate hundreds of ships. An adjacent inlet on the west side of the Bosporus is the Golden Horn.

To the south of Istanbul is The Sea of Marmara that separates the city and ultimately provides a gateway to The Mediterranean Ocean. About 75% of Turkey is surrounded by sea!

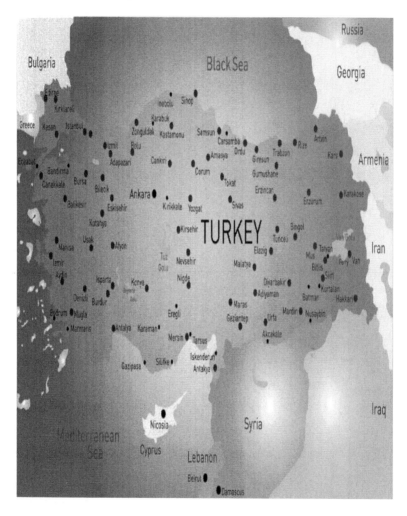

Map of Turkey- Istanbul is on the top left side

A May 2018 online National Geographic article *"Canal Istanbul may displace thousands"* tells of a new canal planned for Turkey near the Istanbul area to divert some of the commercial shipping from the very busy Bosporus strait.

The article goes on to explain that currently there are about 53,000 ships (including thousands of oil tankers) per year that pass through the Bosporus compared to 12,000 ships that use the Panama Canal and 17,000 ships that use the Suez Canal annually.

The new *Canal Istanbul* would also bring major development along the canal with choice real estate that would include shipping yards, luxury homes and a new airport. This airport would have the largest terminal in the world with about 200 million passengers annually! With the eventual addition of *Canal Istanbul* and all of its amenities, the great city of Istanbul will become even greater still especially in regards to sea trade and trade in general. It will be one of the largest world destinations for travelers.

Any city that is not a sea port, especially a major one, cannot be mystery Babylon. This is the reason that Rome cannot be Mystery Babylon. Rome is not a port city as it is located inland from the ocean. More on this important fact will be covered later on in the chapter dealing with Rome. Keep in mind that sea merchants have frequented Istanbul since before it was Constantinople (Byzantium) for millennia.

Another great aspect of world trade in Istanbul is its mighty Grand Bazaar. If you have not heard of the Grand Bazar before, you will probably wonder why not after you learn about it here.

The Grand Bazaar is said to be the world's oldest market venue and one of the world's largest indoor malls. Founded in 1461 as an open market, over the centuries it has grown so that today there are over 4,000 shops there! Imagine this; before Columbus sailed in 1492, this market already existed.

Twenty six streets make up this great market. There are sections of the market specializing in certain merchandise. For example, there is a jewelry section, a carpet section, food vendors and other sections. Vendors who cannot afford the higher priced market stalls there sell their wares beyond the confines of The Grand Bazaar.

Turkey as a whole is known for great craftsmanship in gold. There are gold shops all over the country besides the jewelry section of The Grand Bazaar. One tour book on Turkey I read mentioned that it is common for people there to wear gold bracelets instead of putting money in the banks. This is usually done in 22 carat gold as 24 carat gold is too soft to wear.

In January of 2016, the Museum of Turkish and Islamist Arts had a showcase of pearls and their accessories from around the world as reported in the newspaper, *The Daily Sabah* news.

The list of goods Mystery Babylon deals in, which was covered in Revelation chapter 18, fits Babylon. Historical accounts of Constantinople describe that the city was known to deal in silk, pearls, gold, jewelry, ivory, spices, frankincense and slaves and more. It was one of the places on the ancient "Silk Road" trade routes. It imported silk from China and later on found the way to produce it and exported it.

Even "horses" and "chariots" (Revelation 18:13) fit the description of Constantinople as there were chariot races there in the Hippodrome (equivalent to the Circus Maxus in Rome). Famous statues of four large copper horses were taken from Constantinople in the fourth Crusade and taken away to Italy where they are now found over the entrance of St. Mark's Basilica. These horses are referred to as "The Horses of Saint Mark's."

The Roman Church crusaders on their way to free Jerusalem sacked Eastern Christian Constantinople in 1204. This was a terrible and tragic time when the Western Roman Church attacked the Eastern Church. That is how "The Horses of Saint Mark's" were taken away. In 1261 Constantinople was retaken by the rest of the Byzantine Empire.

The attack on Constantinople caused the Byzantine Empire to be weakened and also degraded Christianity as a result of that. Due to the grandeur, the large population and great trade there, Constantinople was sometimes referred to as the "Queen of Cities" (Revelation 18:7).

Chapter 9- Abominations

In Revelation 17:1-2 it states that "the great harlot who sits on many waters with whom the kings of the earth committed fornication and the inhabitants of the earth were made drunk with the wine of her fornication."

Revelation 17:4 mentions the woman has a golden cup full of abominations and the filthiness of her fornication. Then in the next verse, 5, we read that on her forehead is the name "MYSTERY BABYLON THE GREAT, THE MOTHER OF HARLOTS AND OF THE ABOMINATIONS OF THE EARTH."

It is notable from the previous two passages in Revelation chapter 17 that mystery Babylon spreads her fornication, harlotry and abominations around the world. These sins being talked about are spiritual ones. There are various instances in the Old Testament books of the prophets where the terms adulteries, harlotry and abominations refer to pagan worship to idols and false gods in contrast to devotion to the one true God. This seems to be the case here in Revelation as well.

The one true God is He who created heaven and earth, the God of Abraham, Isaac and Jacob. Just two examples of spiritual harlotry will be given as examples here.

The first is the scripture in Hosea 4:12 that reads, "My people consult their wooden idols, and their diviner's wand informs them. For a spirit of harlotry has led them astray, And they have played the harlot, departing from their God."

Another example is Ezekiel 23: 37, "For they have committed adultery, and blood is on their hands. They have committed adultery with their idols, and even sacrificed their sons whom they bore to Me, passing them through the fire, to devour them."

What spiritual adultery is being spread around the world by Mystery Babylon? Since it is not stated in the passages of scripture one would have to venture a guess. After looking into this area, I would venture to say that it involves forms of celestial worship, past and present specifically rooted in moon worship.

To better understand this, one needs to go back to the beginnings of ancient Istanbul when it was founded as Byzantium by Greeks in 667 B.C. Those Greeks naturally brought their religious culture with them filled with Greek mythology and most notably the adoration of the goddess, Diana.

The famous goddess Diana had many aspects to her for her worshipers ranging from being the goddess of nature, the forest, animals, fertility and the moon. The worship of the goddess Diana had a stronghold in the ancient world. There were other names uses for her in other cultures and places such as the name Artemis.

A variation of her was held in utmost regard in the city of Ephesus mentioned in the book of Acts in chapter 19 from verses 23-36. A riot ensued when Alexander the Coppersmith stirred the people to action against the Apostle Paul and his message against idolatry.

He said that if people continued to turn away from Diana (Artemis) "that the temple of the great goddess Artemis will be discredited and her majesty deposed—she who is worshiped by all the province of Asia and the whole world." When the men heard this, they were enraged and began shouting, "Great is Artemis of the Ephesians," for two hours.

The Temple to Diana in Ephesus was so elaborate that it was considered one of the Seven Wonders of the ancient world. Keep in mind that Ephesus is located in the same country as Istanbul, in Turkey.

I had previously noted that all seven of the churches that the Apostle Paul addressed The Revelation to were all located in Turkey. These churches are first mentioned in Rev 1:11 and are dealt with from there until the end of chapter three.

Close attention should be given to Revelation 2:12-13. There we find out that one of the seven churches Paul addressed was in the city of Pergamum where "Satan's throne is," and "where Satan dwells." It cannot be said with certainty why Satan had a stronghold there but in light of the fact that the world famous worship of Diana and her temple was in the same western part of the country, it is not surprising that this center of spiritual evil was there in Turkey, whose ancient name was Anatolia and is often referred to as Asia Minor.

Centering back on the goddess Diana, it is important to know that one of her symbols was the crescent moon. The 1973 World Book Encyclopedia states in the description of the word CRESCENT that, "the people of Constantinople used the crescent as their symbol. When The Turks conquered the city, they adopted it as their symbol. It appears in the flag of Turkey."

The Turks as Muslims accepted the sign of the crescent moon as theirs and it has since spread to many Muslims around the world. If one looks into the origins of the Muslim religion, one will find a link to celestial worship in the form of moon worship as well.

Various Muslim scholars document that Allah was the name of a preexisting moon god before Mohammed began the Muslim religion. George Braswell Jr. is one such scholar who wrote, "Allah was the god of the local Quarish tribe, which was Mohammed's tribe before he invented Islam to lead his people out of their polytheism. Allah was then known as the Moon God, who had three daughters who were viewed as intercessors for the people into Allah."

Another historian, Vaqqidi, has said Allah was actually the chief of the 360 gods being worshipped in Arabia at the time Mohammed rose to prominence.

Archeology also attests that the name Allah was used in various ancient cultures for a moon god. In his work, *The Archeology of World Religions*, 1952, p482-485, 492, Jack Finegan, writes that, "While Allah is best known as the principal god of Mecca, he was also worshiped in other places throughout Arabia as is shown by the occurrence of the name in Sabean, Minean and particularly Libyanite inscriptions."

For an overview of the origins and errors of the Koran/Quran and more, a must read book is *Islamic Invasion* by Robert A. Morey. There are also various examples of where the Quran contradicts the Bible.

The Bible is written in Hebrew, Greek and a little Aramaic but does not contain any Arabic names for God nor references to Mohammed or the Quran. It is very reliable as history, as archeology and manuscripts such as the Dead Sea scrolls show. The Quran was originally written in Arabic and Mohammed was a Gentile yet Jesus (a Jew who fulfilled various prophecies of the Jewish Old Testament) said in the Gospel of John 4:22 that "salvation is of the Jews."

The closer one goes back to a historical event the more accurate the information about that event tends to be. Likewise, the Bible far predates the Quran (even by thousands of years considering some Old Testament books) therefore attesting that it is more accurate as to what it contains than what the Quran may say on the same subjects. The Quran was not put together as one book, until about 700 years after the New Testament had been written.

It is common for proponents of the Quran to claim that the Bible has been corrupted and therefore not reliable in its content in an attempt to justify the discrepancies between the two books. However, this is really just a claim not backed up by credible evidence. It also has to be considered that worldwide, there is a significant amount of Muslims that cannot read and even less that can read classical Arabic, the touted language of the Quran, thereby not having a familiarity with their own holy book.

The Islamic Educational, Scientific and Cultural Organization (ISESCO) stated that illiteracy rates in the Muslim world ranges between 40 percent among males and 65 percent among females. Some sources relate that the illiteracy rate is higher than that.

Lastly, in Rev 18:23 it mentions about the great city Babylon that, "by your sorcery all the nations were deceived." The Greek work used there for sorcery is *pharmakeia* which means medicine or drugs hence our English word for pharmacy.

If this is a reference to illegal drugs, one needs to only consider that Istanbul is the gateway to Europe and other places for heroin sourced from Southeast Asia and Afghanistan (the main world producer of opium from which heroin is derived).

In reference to legal drugs, then also consider that Turkey is a location for a major local and global corporate pharmaceutical industry doing business with firms and governments in various continents. This drug industry either legal or illegal is also a way that Mystery Babylon spreads its influence.

A summation of this chapter is that Istanbul has been key in the spreading of worldwide religious abominations in the form of ancient pagan religions that have had their basis mainly in moon worship especially through the symbol of the crescent moon. Drug proliferation will also be a significant factor up to the time when the city is destroyed.

Chapter 10- Colors

Part of the description of the woman, which represents the great city (Rev 17:18), is that she is arrayed in "purple and scarlet and fine linen" and deals in them (Rev 17:4, 18:12, 16).

Istanbul is currently known for producing fine linen. There is a notable linen industry there so much so that there is a listing on the Amazon Home & Kitchen website that promotes "The Istanbul Table Cloth" which is described as luxurious linen suitable for use as a wedding tablecloth with a special stain resistant treatment.

Also, there is a weaving tradition in Istanbul where some families of that craft still weave natural and organic material like linen, silk and cotton in a few weaving villages. One Turkish vendor of distinction that uses Turkish artisans, using Turkish fibers to produce unique designs woven on old style looms, is *Jennifer's Haman Distinction*.

The color purple associated with Istanbul is very interesting. There is a political association with the color purple from way back and a physical association that remains to this day.

In the book *Constantinople- Capital of Byzantium* written by Jonathan Harris, who has a doctorate in Byzantine History, he covers the importance of the color purple in that city's history. In the 4th chapter of that book, he relates that by the year 1200 the Great Palace of the Byzantine emperor had become a complex of buildings that included one on the south side of the city overlooking the sea that was known as the Porphyra.

The Porphya contained a notable purple room. The walls of that room were lined with purple marble and purple silk hangings. Since the 8th century that room had been reserved for the Byzantine empresses to bed rest after having had a child, "it could be said that the heir of a reigning emperor was 'Porphyrogenitos' or 'born to the purple' and so earmarked to succeed his father."

Thus, in the history of Istanbul, royalty has been associated with the color purple for centuries and also in one more way. Purple was the color of royal garments for rulers of the Byzantine Empire.

A prized purple dye was used that was derived from certain mollusks. This color was called Tyrian purple which was mostly produced in Tyre, hence the similar name, but later it was also made in Constantinople. Tyrian purple is currently a rare dye and there was an article some years back noting that to make one gram of it, it required 10,000 mollusks and that gram of dye was valued at 2,000 euros.

If one were to visit Istanbul after the springtime blooming season, purple trees could be seen around the city especially on both sides of the Bosporus. These purple leaves come from the Erguvan trees. The Erguvan is sometimes also called the Judas tree as one tradition says it is the kind of tree that Judas, who betrayed Jesus, hanged himself on. While the colors of the leaves vary from shades of pink and red, the most abundant color is purple.

A national newspaper of Turkey, *Daily Sabah*, had an article from April 20, 2014 titled *Istanbul's purple grace* which stated that "The Erguvan tree is unique to Istanbul because there is no other place with more Erguvan trees than Istanbul."

Istanbul had been known for its purple trees since ancient times. To quote further from the above article, "During the Byzantine era, the color of the

Erguvan was regarded as the color and symbol of the empire and its date of establishment corresponded to the Erguvan's bloom (the month of May)."

This now brings us to the color scarlet. In a previous chapter, it was covered that the flag of Constantinople which was later adopted by the Ottoman Empire and then some Muslim counties, contained the symbol of the crescent moon. The main color of that flag was red or scarlet. Today the national flag of Turkey is about the same with a scarlet background and a white crescent moon with a five pointed star. So, it can be said that the color scarlet which had its origin as a city flag for Constantinople still bears that color today as Istanbul.

The national anthem of Turkey refers to their scarlet flag especially in its first line which reads, "Fear not; for the crimson banner that proudly ripples in this glorious dawn, shall not fade, before the last fiery hearth that is ablaze within my homeland is extinguished."

Chapter 11- Rome

The specific identity of Mystery Babylon is not revealed in the scripture. One is left with an assortment of clues as in a connect- the- dot puzzle and connecting all of the clues as dots covered in this work, reveals a clear picture of Istanbul being Mystery Babylon.

The main clues; a great city, a location on 7 hills, a false religious influence and a world renown sea port, matches the city of Istanbul. Those main clues and all the other minor ones explained in this body of work only bolster that conclusion.

However, I must cover more in depth here why Rome is the main city often picked as Mystery Babylon. It matches most of the main clues especially being known as a great city, being built on 7 hills and has a history of Christian persecution.

About all of the people who support Rome being Mystery Babylon also focus on the spiritual abominations mentioned in Revelation as relating to the Roman Catholic Church which has had Rome as its headquarters from when the Roman Empire adopted Christianity as a state religion in the 4th century.

Rome was the city where the Roman Catholic Church was founded hence its name. Rome also was an early persecutor of the Christian Church under the Roman Empire which had Jesus crucified and many of his followers rounded up and killed. Many people have heard of Christians being thrown to the lions in the Coliseum back then.

That Roman church also has a bloody history of persecuting and killing other Christians as in the Spanish Inquisition where thousands of people were put to death as heretics for not accepting papal rule or violating what was considered other serious infractions of that church.

I already covered how that church also sacked Constantinople and the Eastern Orthodox Church there also killing Christians there in large numbers raping and pillaging in that city.

Besides that, there are other beliefs and practices of that church that are held to be in error which have been traditional views of historical Protestantism. I won't go into that here as it would take too much time. Anyone interested in that subject can consider the 95 theses of Martin Luther which he promoted in 1517 in an attempt to bring reform to that church.

The one abomination I will point out is the Roman Catholic Church requirement that its priests and nuns be celibate. This is putting a heavy burden on people that they cannot often carry resulting in various sexual scandals. The Bible expressly states that any teaching that prohibits marriage is a "doctrine of demons" (1 Timothy 4:1-3) and that not all people can be celibate but to be so is a gift from God (I Corinthians 7: 6-10). The Apostle Paul was single during his apostleship.

What most people fail to understand is that the current Roman Catholic Church is no longer a part of Rome even though it still bears that name. In 1929 Benito Mussolini signed the Lateran Treaty which dissolved the Papal States or territory that the Roman Church controlled in Italy, except for granting that the Vatican State (The Vatican) could remain as the property for that church.

While technically located within Rome in Italy, The Vatican is a sovereign city state under control by the

Pope. That also means it is its own country with its own national anthem and flag.

The Vatican is named after Vatican Hill which also disqualifies it and the Roman Catholic Church from being Mystery Babylon as it is currently located on only one hill and not on seven.

For those who insist that the city of Rome is Mystery Babylon, I will remind them here that that city itself is not a seaport and definitely not a world class one either. There is no way around this important fact.

Rome is located about 18 miles from the Tyrrhenian Sea (part of the Mediterranean Ocean) and does have the Tiber River flowing through it to the sea but it is not deep enough to support any international shipping which requires "deep water" ports. Those are ports with at least a water depth of 30 feet or more. A Regular port is considered 20 feet deep or less and is used mostly for recreational boats.

A bridge over the Tiber River in Rome

The Tiber River ranges from a depth of just 7 to 20 feet. Also, bridges that cross the Tiber have arches that would not allow for larger commercial ships to pass through. These are stone block bridges not enormous expansion bridges that can open up and elevate a section to allow huge ships to pass through.

You may hear of there being "the port of Rome." That is the city of Civitavecchia which serves as a port for Rome but is located about 40 miles northwest of Rome. It's at least 1.5 hours by taxi or bus or 45 minutes by train. The population there is about 53,000. It is considered a "seaport" of "Medium" port size by the International shipping organization "SeaRates" not a larger Deepwater Seaport. It is a common cruise ship destination.

Civitavecchia is considered a "commune" of Rome which means it is a municipality of Rome. Legally it belongs to Rome but to say that it meets the biblical requirement that Rome be an international seaport would be really stretching the point. There are almost 8,000 "comuni" in Italy headed by a mayor and a ruling council. These are smaller cities in themselves.

Whenever I have read some written work citing Rome as Mystery Babylon, or any other city for that matter, it ignores any commentary on its relationship to shipping and the sea as the Revelation describes. Nobody seems to notice this main clue from the biblical narrative is missing in that content. This important aspect to Mystery Babylon is a game changer for those who have held the traditional Rome view.

To miss in scripture that Mystery Babylon is a world class seaport is to miss the mark greatly.

Conclusion

When I first came across the major clue that Istanbul, which is known in history mostly as Constantinople, was located on 7 hills, I looked into this. Sure enough, it was the case. As I searched further, I was very surprised that I did not find any online sources or articles giving the conclusion that Istanbul is Mystery Babylon.

My only guess for this is that mostly everybody has just accepted that Rome was the great city in question. Why look for another place when you are so sure you have found it? This also means that my written work here is very original and so I realize it will not be accepted by some who will go with the popular view even though it does not meet every main clue as I covered. Some people will not accept this view no matter what. Breaking with tradition is not always easy.

Another reason some people will reject "the Istanbul view" is that they will trust too much in their Bible teachers or preachers and to accept that Mystery Babylon is Istanbul will infer that those people are mistaken. Blind trust or loyalty will sometimes not allow for independent thinking. We would all do well to be as the noble minded Bereans that are mentioned in the book of Acts who read the scriptures for themselves to see if something was true (Acts 17:11).

Some Bible reference books clearly state that Rome is Mystery Babylon without even proving the point and others just tie it to the 7 hills also contributing to that view and present it as forgone conclusion.

Let me make one thing clear here, I am not prophesying here only giving my best understanding of the location that fulfils the prophetic vision that the Apostle John gave to the churches about Mystery Babylon that he was shown by one of God's angels.

It is my hope that any student of prophecy will welcome this book as a serious work to be evaluated based on the scriptures and the record of history. The country of Turkey should also bear more scrutiny as it will have a part to play near the very end of times.

I hope that this book will also serve to be an alert to millions of people that are in Istanbul and even the rest of Turkey so that they will know beforehand that a great destruction is coming and that they will understand to flee when the time comes. May they recognize that God has spoken in the Bible to warn any who would listen about this terrible event that will come and realize that He has sent his son, Jesus, to provide forgiveness of sins and a way to heaven by trusting in Him as the only savior for their sins.

Keep in mind that the book of Revelation promises a blessing to those who read and heed it (Rev 1:3). Be blessed and read that book if you haven't already even if some things in it are hard to understand.

About The Author

When I was 20 years old I converted to being a follower of Jesus the Christ. The word Christ is Greek for the word Messiah which literally means "the anointed one."

I have been a Christian for at least 38 years now and have regularly read and studied the Bible in all that time including currently now reading it from beginning to the end for the 15th time.

About a year ago I published my first fiction book *Tell Tale Tracks* as an e-book. It is a story based on real existing dinosaur and human tracks found together in the same strata presented in a museum discovery setting. I hope to format it as a movie script later on.

Istanbul Is Mystery Babylon is my first work of non-fiction. I have several other biblically related books I plan to write as well. I am a native of Reno, Nevada in the U.S. A.